An Illustrated ABC Book
from the students of
Columbus College of Art and Design

Letters of the Legendary: An Illustrated ABC Book
ISBN: 978-1522735212

Cover illustration by Sarah Moore.
Edited by Adam Osgood and Rebecca Zomchek.

The illustrations in this book were created by the students of
Illustration for Graphic Design, taught by Rebecca Zomchek and
Adam Osgood. Biographical text and information is borrowed and
adapted from Wikipedia under the Creative Commons License.

To think. To do. To reflect.
To unleash your power to shape culture and commerce.

Columbus College of Art & Design
60 Cleveland Avenue, Columbus, OH 43215
www.ccad.edu

"Action, looks, words, steps, form the alphabet by which you may spell character."

— Johann Kaspar Lavater (German Theologian, 1741-1801)

his book is a collection of Drop Cap* examples from the Columbus College of Art and Design's *Illustration for Graphic Design*** and *Illustration Capstone**** classes of 2015. Hand lettering is a fantastic example of the beautiful harmony that can work between traditional art skills and graphic design.

This year students in both classes were challenged to develop illustrative drop cap designs based on famous figures who have contributed to society or impacted history. The designers researched their chosen figures by collecting written and visual data about their lives; including details about their origins, education, location, careers and achievements. Using this research, the students created illustrations highlighting each figure's memorable and distinctive qualities, capturing glimpses into the lives and accomplishments of the highlighted individuals.

This is Columbus College of Art and Design's third printed collection of the Drop Cap project and the students have put together an excellent compendium of work showcasing multiple styles and artistic problem solving. We hope to continue this tradition and level of design work for years to come.

–Rebecca Zomchek & Adam Osgood
Assistant Professors, Illustration Department, CCAD

*Drop Cap: In book publishing the first letter of a paragraph that is enlarged to "drop" down two or more lines. Drop caps are often seen at the beginning of novels, where the top of the first letter of the first word lines up with the top of the first sentence and drops down to the four or fifth sentence to the beginning of a section (webopedia.com). Or: A large, often highly decorated letter set at the beginning of a chapter, verse, or paragraph (thefreedictionary.com).

***Illustration for Graphic Design* introduces graphic design students the power of visual storytelling and exposes them to the process of picture making from the perspective of an illustrator.

****Senior Illustration Capstone* prepares students for future careers as illustrators, challenging them to develop their personal style while building a complete portfolio of work.

Edwin Eugene "Buzz" Aldrin (1930–present)

American engineer and former astronaut, and the second
person to walk on the Moon. He was the Lunar Module Pilot
on Apollo 11, the first manned lunar landing in history.

Kati Jenkins

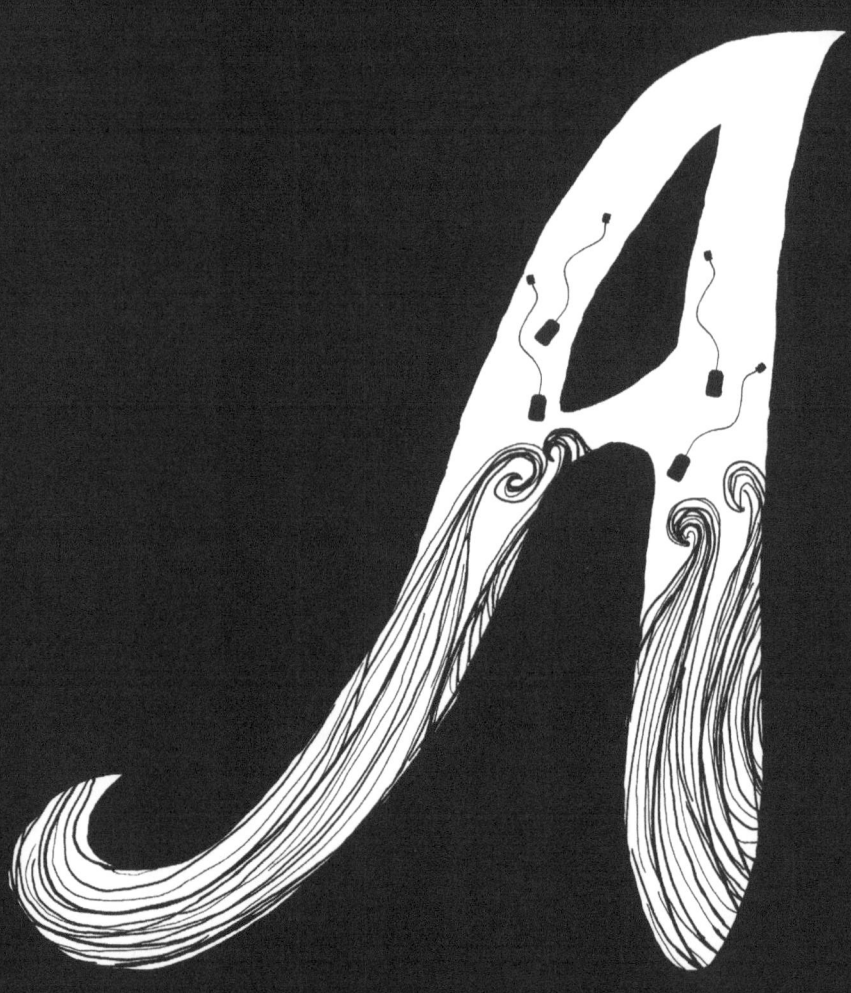

John Adams (1735–1826)

American lawyer, author, statesman, and diplomat. He served as the second President of the United States, the first Vice President, and as a Founding Father was a leader of American independence from Great Britain.

Alyssa Kash

Paul Brown (1908-1991)

American football coach in the All-America Football Conference and NFL. Brown was the first coach of the Cleveland Browns, a team named after him, and later played a role in founding the Cincinnati Bengals.

Joe Gemma

John Baird (1888–1946)

Scottish engineer, innovator, one of the inventors of the mechanical television.
He shorted the city of Glasgow's power trying to create diamonds with electricity.

Brandon Shrader

Joseph A. Campbell (1817-1900)

Creator of Campbell's Soup, which first introduced tomato soup in 1897. By 1905, the company offered 21 different varieties. It has now become a household item that everyone is familiar with.

Ashten Justus

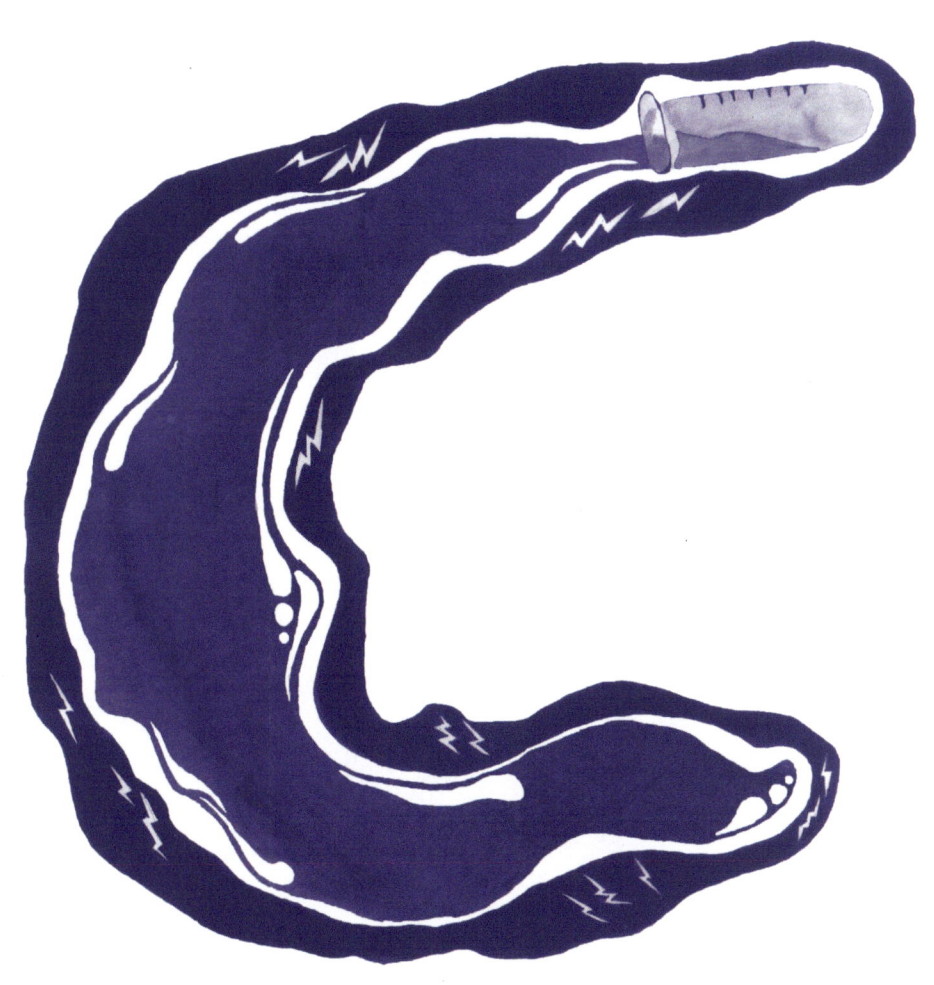

Marie Curie (1867–1934)

Polish and naturalized-French physicist and chemist
who conducted pioneering research on radioactivity.
"Nothing in life is to be feared; it is only to be understood."

Heidi Clifford

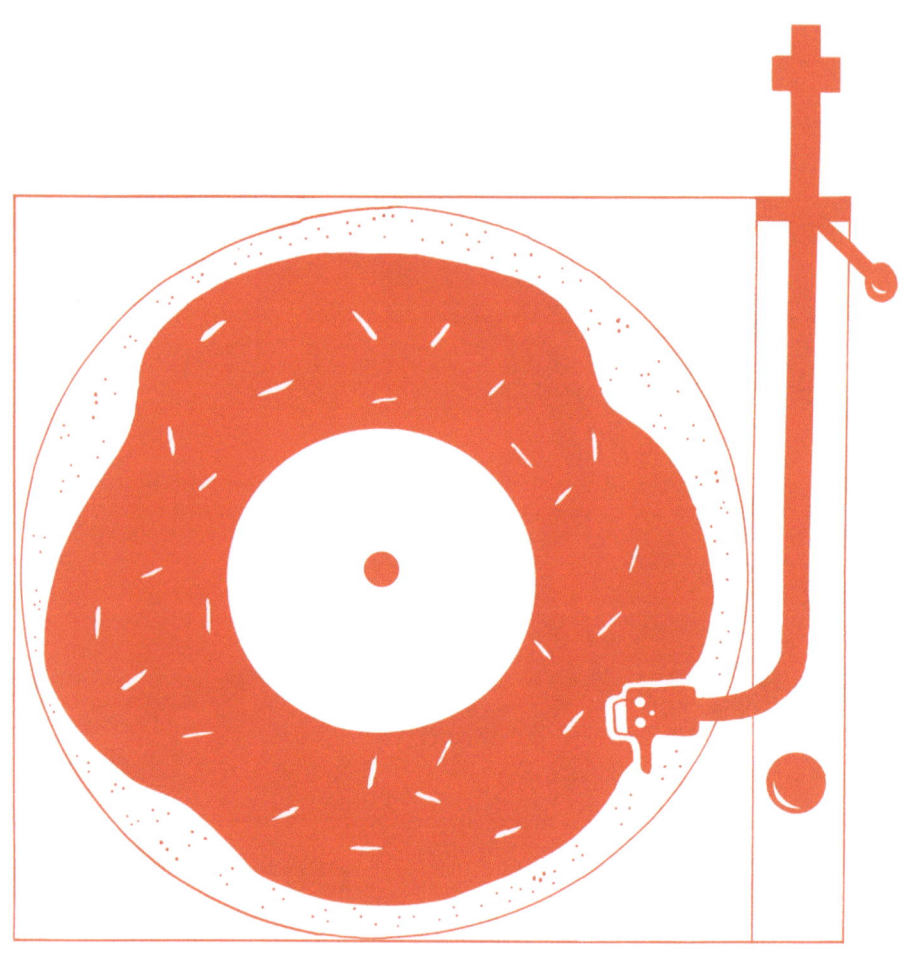

J Dilla (1974-2006)

American record producer and rapper who emerged from the mid-1990s underground hip hop scene in Detroit, Michigan. He was an influential hip-hop artist, working with big-name acts including A Tribe Called Quest, De La Soul, Busta Rhymes, Erykah Badu, The Roots, and Common.

Joe Gemma

Charles Darwin (1809–1882)

English naturalist and geologist who was also a scientific explorer. Founded the biological theory of evolution.

Brandon Shrader

Leif Erikson (c. 970–1020)

Icelandic explorer credited by some as being the first European
to land in North America before Christopher Columbus.

Nicole Cmar

Isabelle Eberhardt (1877–1904)

Swiss explorer and writer who traveled from Switzerland to Algeria. Identified as a male called Si Mahmoud Essadi and published short stories under that name.

Haley Kidder

Philo Farnsworth (1906–1971)

American inventor who was instrumental in the early development
in the electronic television. He invented the first fully functional
all-electronic image pickup device or video camera.

Sunny Ngo

Robert Frost (1874–1963)

American poet who specialized in depicting rural life in New England
while examining complex social and philosophical themes.

Sarah Moore

Galileo Galilei (1564–1642)

Italian astronomer, physicist, engineer, philosopher and mathematician who took part in many aspects of the scientific revolution during the Renaissance. He is remembered for his controversial heliocentric views.

Grace Anderson

Emma Goldman (1869–1940)

Anarchist, political activist, and philosopher. She was key in developing much of the anarchist ideologies that are still relevant today.

Haley Kidder

Attila the Hun (406–453)

The fierce ruler of the Hunnic Empire, a tribal confederation
consisting of Huns, Ostrogoths, and Alans among others,
on the territory of Central and Eastern Europe.

Shawn Thomas

Audrey Hepburn (1929–1993)

British actress and humanitarian who is well known for her talent and beauty.

Sarah Moore

Steve Irwin (1962–2006)

Nicknamed "The Crocodile Hunter", was an Australian wildlife
expert, television personality, and conservationist.

Alyssa Kash

Queen Isabella I (1451–1504)

Most well known for sponsoring Columbus' 1492 voyage and
the uniting Castile and Aragon to become Spain.

Catherine Norwood

Joan of Arc (1412–1431)

After receiving spiritual visions from above, Joan left her quiet life as a peasant and stepped up to the role as "the savior of France," joining the French Army at age 17 and leading her fellow troops to an attack during the Hundred Year War.

Catherine Norwood

Steve Jobs (1955–2011)

The co-founder, chairman and chief executive officer of Apple Inc. Jobs
is widely recognized as a pioneer of the microcomputer revolution
of the 1970s, along with Apple co-founder Steve Wozniak.

Justin Woomin Jeong

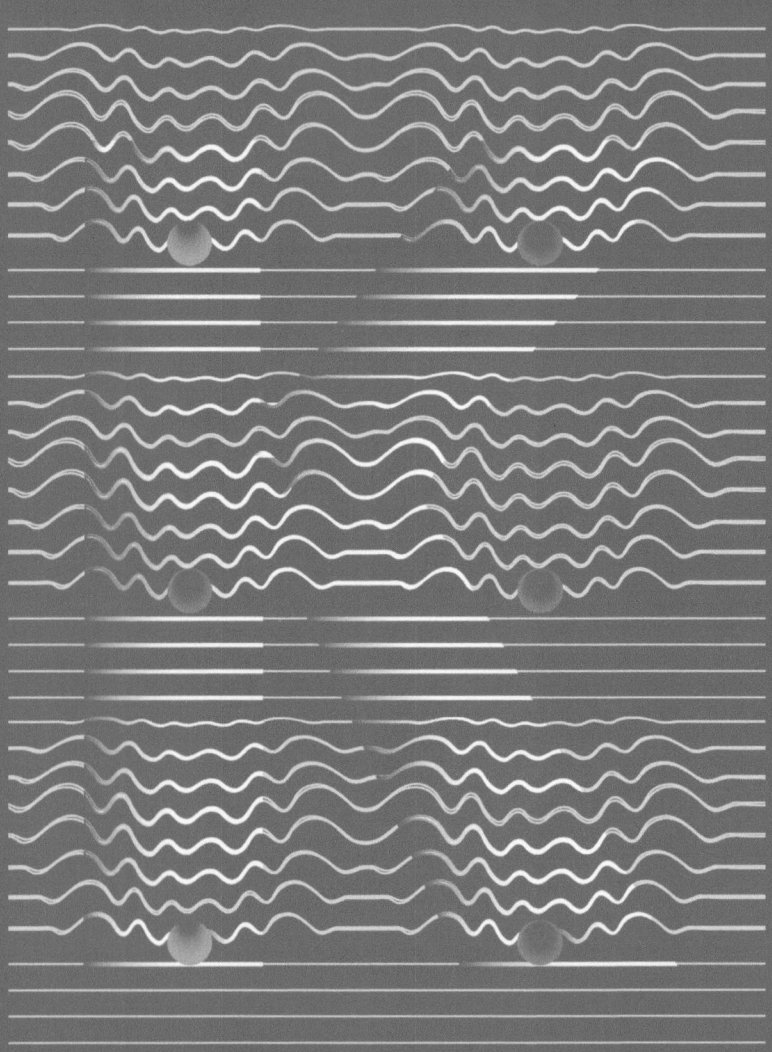

Helen Keller (1880–1968)

One of the world's most influential humanitarians of all time, Keller lead an
inspiring life while overcoming the challenges of being deaf and blind.

Catherine Norwood

Rudyard Kipling (1865–1936)

English author of short stories, poems, and children's literature. His tales and poems of India continue to excite the imagination of today's readers.

Hannah Williams

Abraham Lincoln (1809–1865)

The 16th President of the United States, Lincoln served through the
Civil War; preserving the Union, abolishing slavery, strengthening
the federal government, and modernizing the economy.

Justin Woomin Jeong

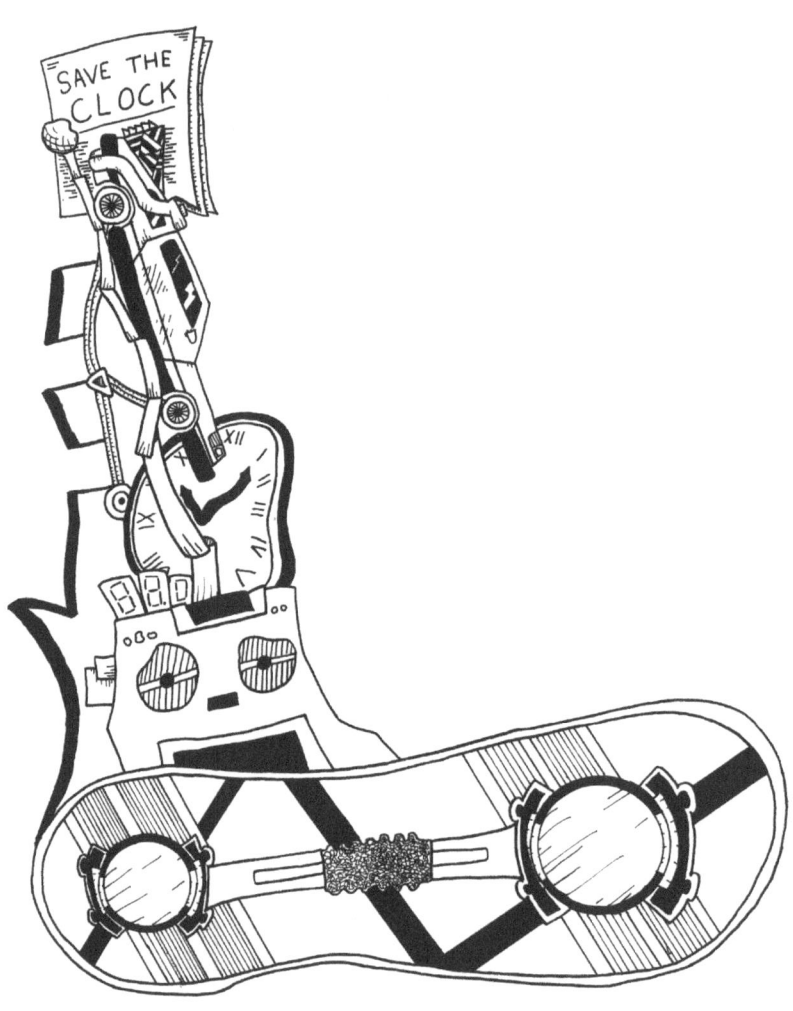

Christopher Allen Lloyd (1938–present)

American actor whose most notable roles include Emmett "Doc" Brown from the *Back to the Future film* series, Uncle Fester from *The Addams Family* movies, and Commander Kruge from *Star Trek*.

Teodoro Viera

Winsor McCay (1869–1934)

American cartoonist and animator. He is best known for the comic strip *Little Nemo* and the animated film *Gertie the Dinosaur*.

Juan Argil

Freddy Mercury (1946–1991)

British singer, songwriter and producer, best known as the lead vocalist and songwriter of the rock band Queen. As a performer, he was known for his flamboyant stage persona and powerful vocals over a four-octave range.

Teodoro Viera

Sir Isaac Newton (1643–1727)

A genius known for developing differential calculus and the study of
about optics. He was the first to build the reflecting telescope.

Katherine Jennings

Florence Nightingale (1820–1910)

The "Lady with the Lamp" was an English pioneer of professional nursing who became a force of change for healthcare reform worldwide.

Anna D'Amico

George Orwell (1903–1950)

British novelist, journalist, and critic. His work was known for supporting democratic socialism and spreading awareness of social injustice.

Anna-Lisa Eriksson

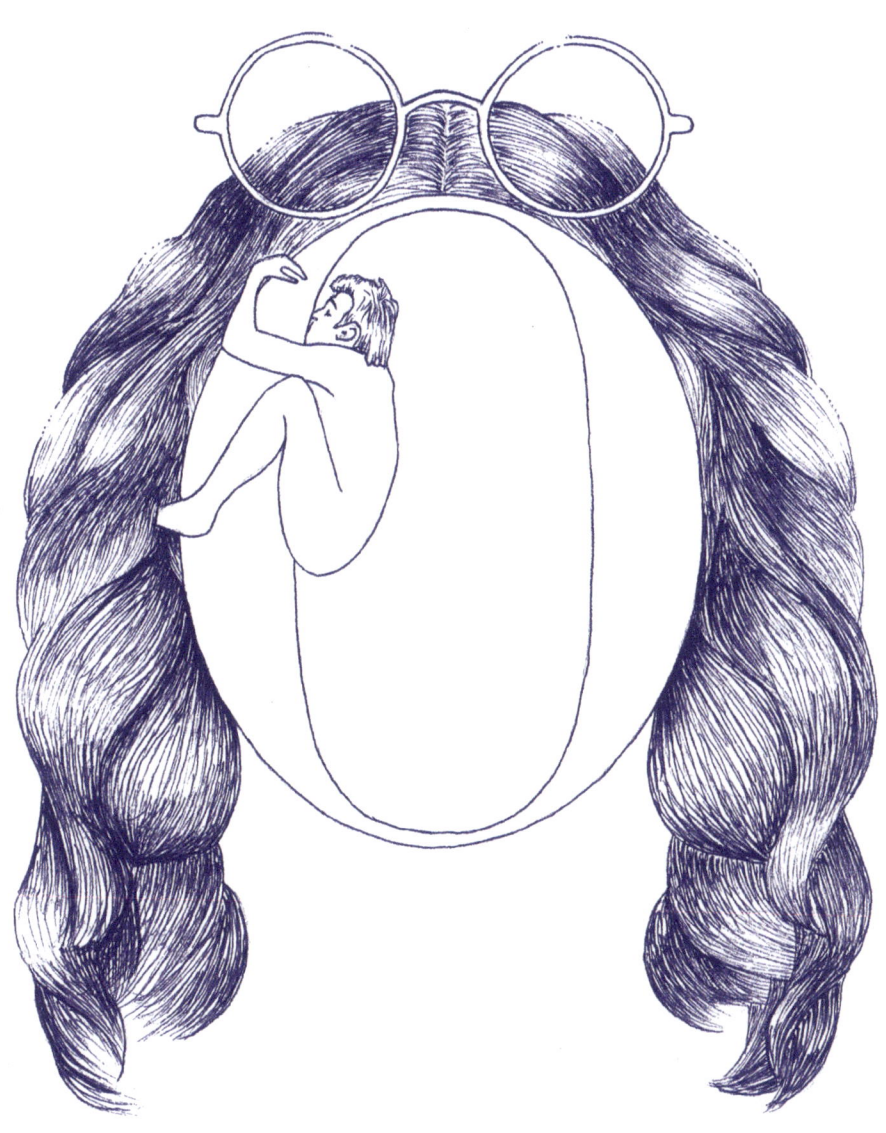

Yoko Ono (1933–present)

Japanese artist and musician who was an influential practitioner of conceptual and performance art in the 1960s. She was the wife of John Lennon.

Katherine Jennings

Edgar Allan Poe (1809–1849)

American writer, editor, and literary critic. Poe is best known
for his poetry and short stories, particularly his tales of mystery
and the macabre, including *The Tell-Tale Heart.*

Alysia Scherger

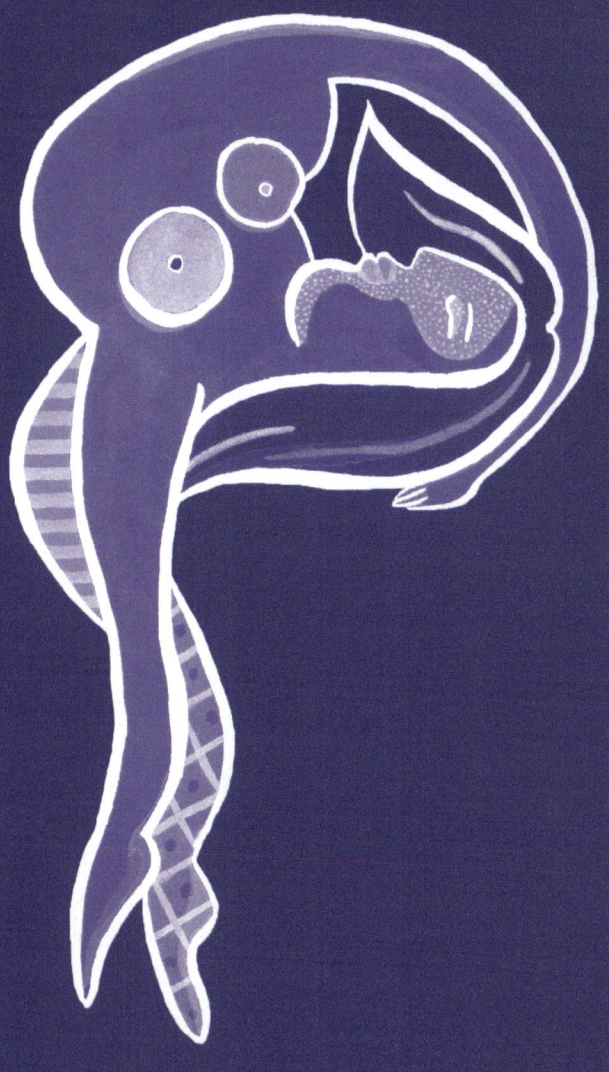

Pablo Picasso (1881–1973)

Picasso laid the basic foundations of modern art. He went beyond
the ways of expressionism, breaking down his figures in a series of
distorted geometric shapes. He painted in a cubist manner.

Katherine Jennings

Roxanne Quimby (1950–present)

Roxanne Quimby is an American businesswoman notable for founding the Burt's Bees personal care products company with beekeeper Burt Shavitz.

Emilie Brosnan

Kellin Quinn (1986–present)

The versatile lead vocalist for the band Sleeping With Sirens.
Born on April 24th, 1986 in Oregon, he began his singing career
with a band called Closer 2 Closure before gaining fame.

Shane Richardson

Herman Rorschach (1884–1922)

Swiss psychiatrist and psychoanalyst, best known for developing
a test known as the Rorschach inkblot test, designed to reflect
unconscious parts of the personality that project onto the stimuli.

Jonathan Pritt

Erno Rubik (1944–Present)

Architect and Professor of Architecture, he is best known as the inventor of the Rubiks Cube in 1974. He taught at the Budapest University of Technology from 1962-1967 and the Hungarian Academy of Applied Arts from 1967-1971.

Shane Richardson

Mary Wollstonecraft Shelley (1797–1851)

English novelist, essayist, biographer, and travel writer best
known for writing the Gothic novel *Frankenstein*.

Alicia Weninger

Elaine Stritch (1925–2014)

American actress and singer, best known for her work on Broadway. The only thing bigger than her career was her bold, brassy, larger-than-life attitude.

Lindsey Kaufman

Tomoyuki Tanaka (1910–1997)

Creator and producer of the Godzilla series. These films and their interpretations have led an eccentric generation of giant monster movies and millions of fans in their following.

Mitch Hawk

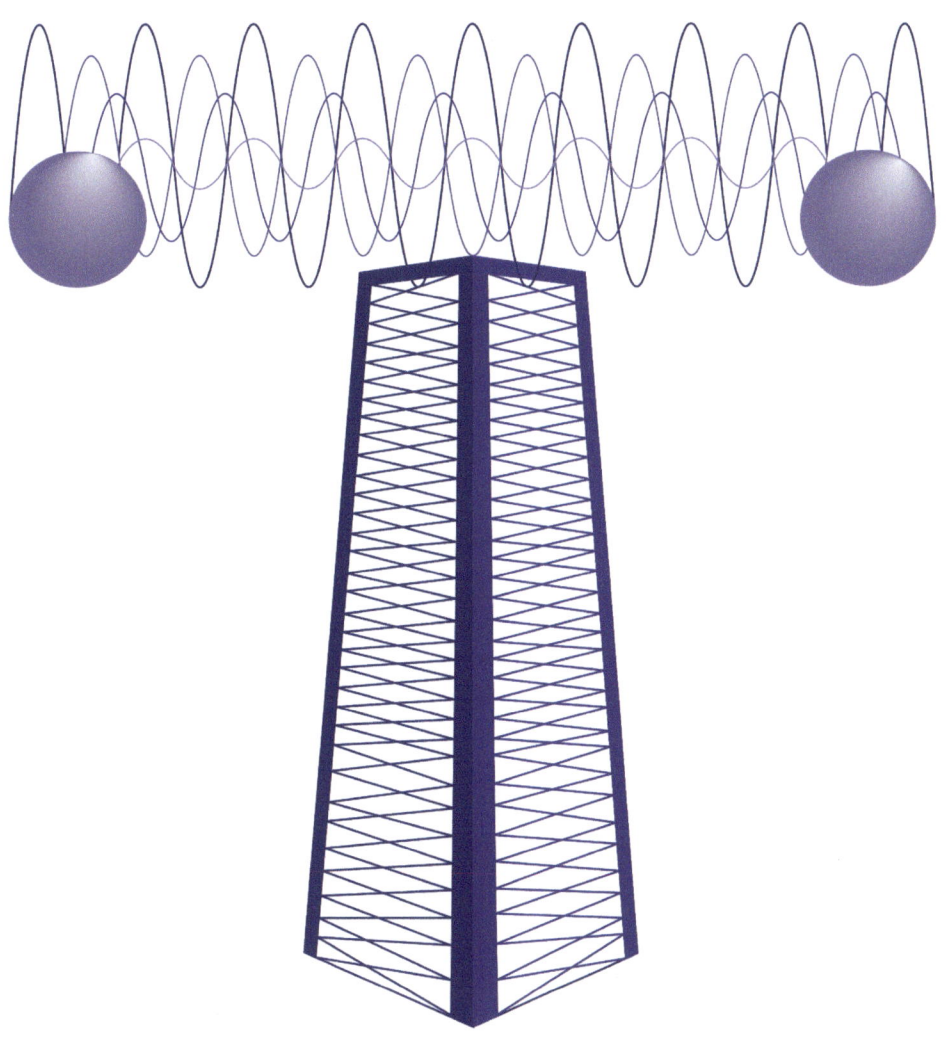

Nikola Tesla (1856–1943)

Serbian-American inventor, electrical engineer, mechanical engineer, physicist, and futurist best known for his contributions to the design of the modern alternating current (AC) electricity supply system.

Rafael Fernandez

Kazuo Umezu (1936–present)

Comic Artist who pioneered the horror manga genre.

Alissa Sallah

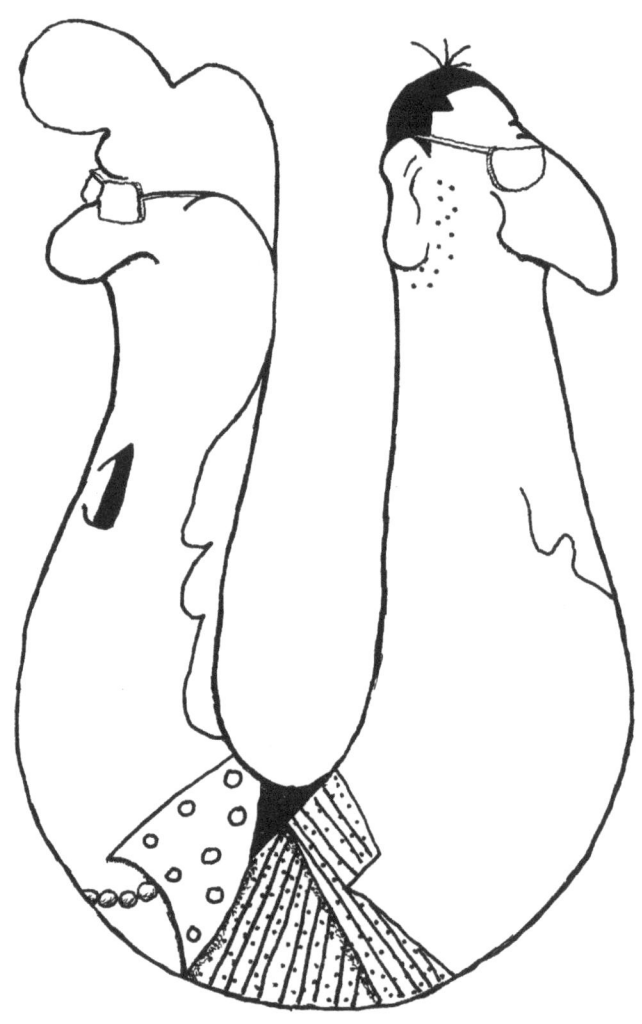

Jim Unger (1937–2012)

British-Canadian cartoonist best known for his syndicated comic-strip *Herman* featured in more than 600 newspapers for eighteen years. This quirky comic showcased Unger's sense of humor.

Cory Wilcox

Gianni Versace (1946–1997)

Italian fashion designer and founder of Versace, an international
fashion house known for its decadent style.

Heidi Clifford

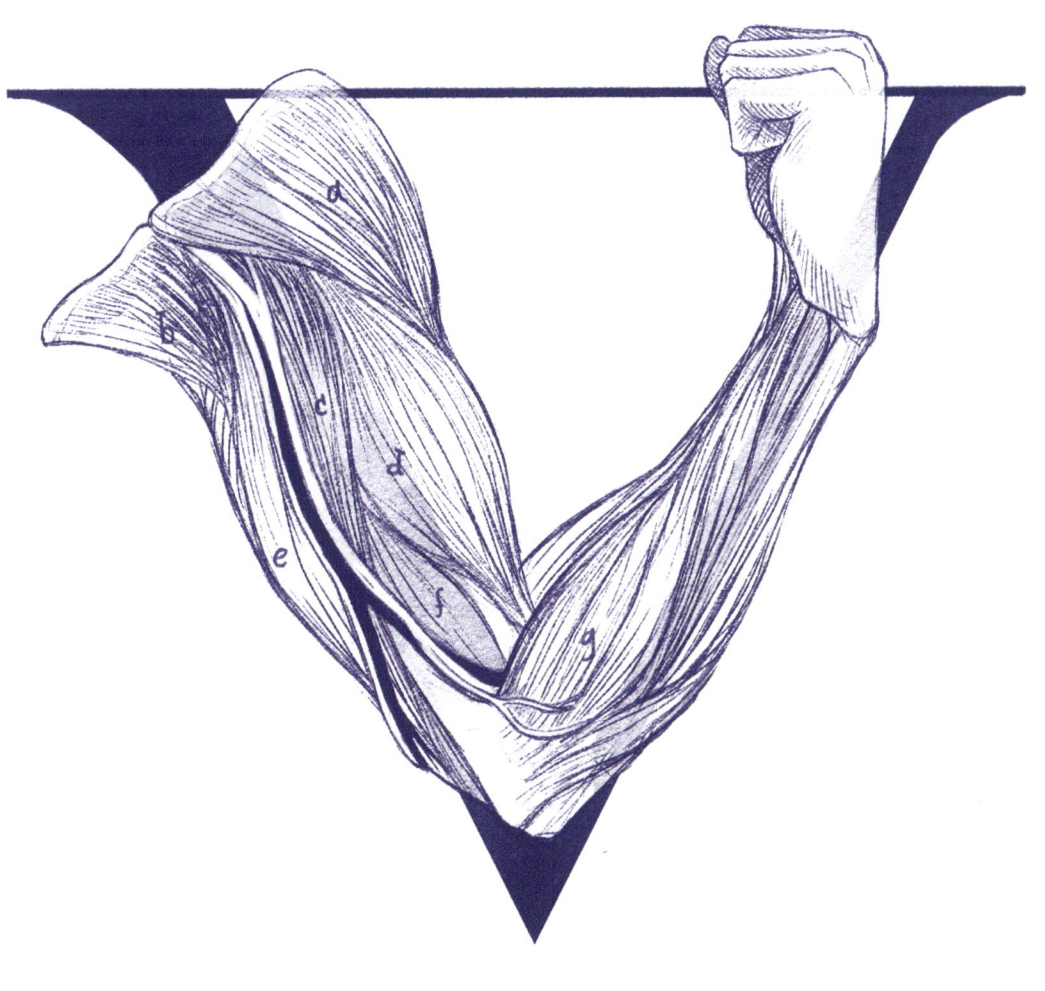

Andreas Vesalius (1514–1564)

A founder of modern human anatomy, he was one of the first physicians allowed to dissect and document the body. He is the author of *De humani corporis fabrica (On the Fabric of the Human Body)*.

K. Fedorco

Andy Warhol (1928–1987)

American artist who was a leading figure in the visual art movement known as pop art. His works explore the relationship between artistic expression, celebrity culture, and advertisement that flourished by the 1960s.

Sarah Moore

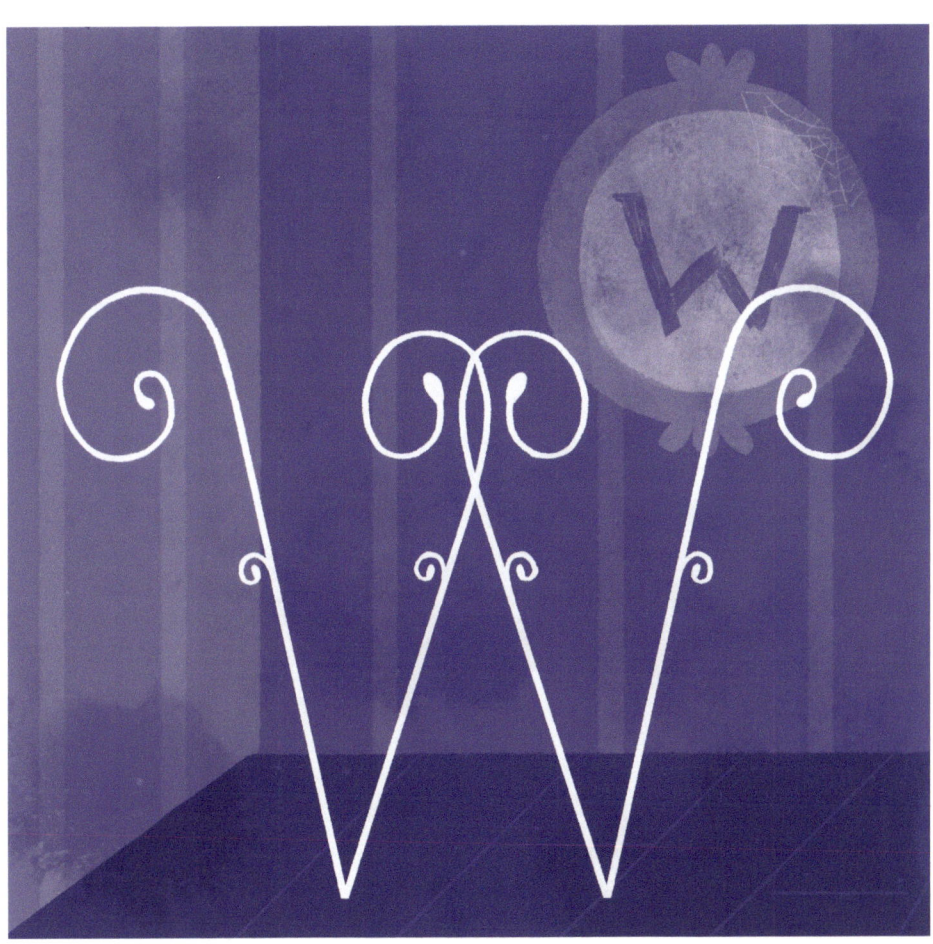

Oscar Wilde (1854–1900)

Irish playwright, novelist, essayist and poet. Wilde was one of London's
most popular and influential playwrights in the late 1800's.

Cat Tervo

Malcolm X (1925–1965)

Born Malcolm Little and also known as el-Hajj Malik el-Shabazz,
he was a Human rights activist and American Muslim minister.
"Be peaceful, be courteous, obey the law, respect everyone; but if
someone puts his hand on you, send him to the cemetery."

Christopher Passabet

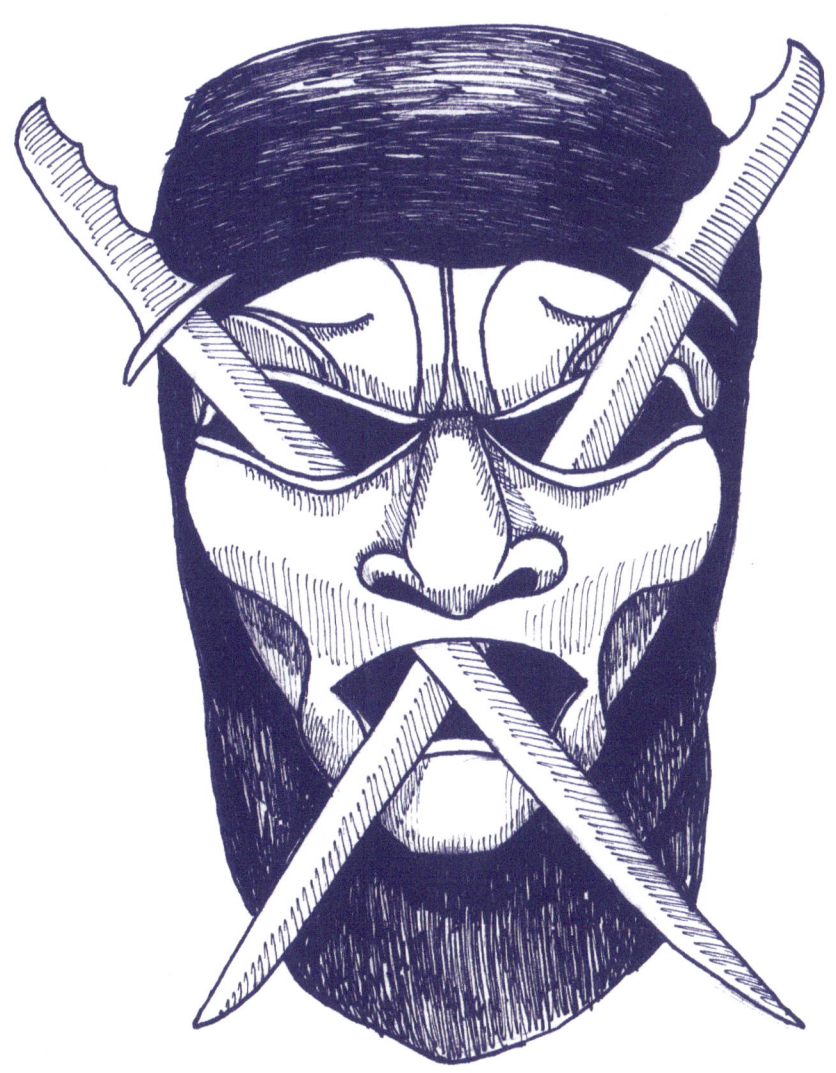

Xerxes the Great (519–466 BC)

Xerxes I of Persia, also known as Xerxes the Great, was the fourth of the king of kings of the Achaemenid Empire. He ruled from 486 BC until his assassination in 465 BC at the hands of Artabanus, the commander of the royal bodyguard.

Ian Adams

Chic Young (1910–1973)

Murat Bernard Young, better known as Chic Young, was an American
cartoonist who created the popular, long-running comic strip *Blondie.*

Alyssa Kash

John Zachary Young (1907–1997)

English zoologist and neurophysiologist who was known for his research on the nervous system. Most of his work focused on cephalopods (octopus, squid, cuttlefish and the nautilus).

Kit Mizeres

Ferdinand von Zeppelin (1838–1917)

German general, dirigible pioneer, and founder of the Zeppelin airship company.

Logan Schmitt

Mark Zuckerberg (1984–present)

Cofounder of the social networking website Facebook, developed while he was a student at Harvard University. He is now considered among the 100 wealthiest and most influential people in the world before the age of 30.

Elizabeth Cansfield

Ian Adams (Xerxes)
ianadams182@gmail.com, about.me/ianadams182

"The best part about being an artist is seeing the beauty in the things around. Not just seeing objects as objects or the landscapes around me as just landscapes, but seeing the intricacy and delicacy in each thing. I'm able to appreciate the world around me and get inspired to create something of my own, and it's nice having a natural talent to be able to do so when I want to create something of my own. "

Juan Manuel Argil Aguilar (Winsor McCay)
juan@thatjuanartist.com, thatjuanartist.com

On being an artist: "The best thing about being an artist is being able to communicate abstract thoughts to others."

On inspiration: "Making work that informs other people of issues they may not know about within known situations."

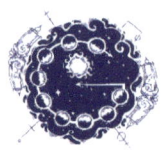

Grace Elizabeth Anderson (Galileo Galilei)
ganderson.2@go.ccad.edu

"My favorite thing about design and illustration is creating artwork with the purpose of catching people's eye, and seeing people's reactions to the work. I am most inspired to do my best work when I look at works by other artists. When I see a great piece it drives me because I believe if I work hard enough my own work can get better."

Emilie Brosnan (Roxanne Quimby)
brosnanemilie@gmail.com, behance.net/Emilie_Brosnan

"What inspires me to do my best work is my family. When my family has a goal or something they want to achieve they do everything possible to make that goal and this has been my goal sense my freshman year at high school, so I will do everything and everything just to say I have done my best work."

Liz Cansfield (Mark Zuckerberg)
ecansfield.1@go.ccad.edu, behance.com/lizcansfield

"Graphic design and illustration are mutually beneficial to each other. Both are means of visual communication, and having both of those skills helps you as an artist to convey your ideas more effectively. Especially recently there has been a lot of overlap between the two fields. Most of my work incorporates illustration in some way; it can really enhance a project."

Heidi Clifford (Marie Curie, Gianni Versace)
hlclifford94@gmail.com, behance.net/heidiclifford

"The greatest inspiration to me that has influenced my best work has consistently been those around me, as well as artists and designers that I have researched, that tend to put a bit of themselves into their work. I find that I most love my work and projects when I can really put myself into them and make them personally relevant."

Nicole Cmar (Leif Erikson)
nicolecmar@gmail.com, nicolecmar.com

On inspiration: "Taking a drive, reading Shel Silverstein, or watching anything Jim Henson will always do the trick. Soft rock and other random music inspires me a lot too. I have a huge variety I listen to, including the Velvet Underground, John and Yoko, Belle and Sebastian, Pink Floyd, Tom Waits, random French music, 50's rock, or maybe even Tiny Tim. I'm kinda all over the place."

Anna D'Amico (Florence Nightingale)
a.damico@me.com, adamicoart.com

"My favorite thing about design and illustration is the ability to tell stories in a visual medium. Aspiring to be able to get to the point where I can clearly communicate the images I see in my head onto paper and be pleased with my work is what inspires me most."

Anna-Lisa Eriksson (George Orwell)
annalisamarika.art@gmail.com, annalisaeriksson.com

"My favorite thing about design and illustration is that it gives harmony to everything. Without design and illustration, it would be a different world. I am always inspired to create something new and unique. The possibilities are endless when it comes to illustrating your thoughts onto paper. It is important to me that my audience has never seen anything like it before."

K. Fedorco (Andreas Vesalius)
KFedorco.1@go.ccad.edu, behance.net/KFedorco

"Illustration is fascinating because it allows any subject to become tangible in a narrative space. Regardless of the "type" of illustration—comics, editorial vignettes, concept development, drawing or painting—art is a human experience, and being able to communicate a complex concept with an image is absolutely incredible."

Rafael Fernandez III (Nikola Tesla)
rafael.fdez03@gmail.com, behance.net/rfernandez03

"Favorite thing about design and illustration: Being able to give a design the personal touch by either a hand lettered message, or by simply experimenting with different techniques and mediums to get a great piece of work that isn't solely digital. Inspiration for my best work comes from multiple places. Beginning with my culture, my love for music, food, and trying new things, all through being innovative, and finding out different avenues to push new concepts and ideas for my work to travel on and be impactful."

Joe Gemma (Paul Brown, J Dilla)
JoeDGemma@Gmail.com, behance.net/JoeDgemma

"Being able to convey an idea or message without always having to use words can be a very powerful thing and one of my favorite aspects of design and illustration. There are countless languages in the world, but shapes and images are understood globally, which makes them an exciting medium to convey my thoughts and ideas."

Mitch Hawk (Tomoyuki Tanaka)
me@mitchwhawk.com, mitchwhawk.com

"I think the best part about this profession is being able to do new and interesting work every other week. It's more fun when you can see your work getting better as you progress and become more familiar with the work in your niche."

Kati Jenkins (Buzz Aldrin)
seylent@gmail.com, behance.net/katijenkins

"My favorite thing about being an artist is having this exclusive little window of opportunity to look, not only inside myself but also into other artist's lives. No matter how simple or seemingly straightforward the piece is, there is always a reason you draw something a certain way, there's a comforting flow behind the process, there is a deeper meaning behind that motif. Even if you're being paid to do it , it's a part of you, you have control, and there's something of you in there."

Kat Jennings (Isaac Newton, Yoko Ono, Pablo Picasso)
Kat_Jennings@mac.com, behance.net/kaatyvonne

"Being an artist gives you the opportunity to express yourself and self-promote in ways that can catch the eye of someone much faster than any other sort of exhibition. It's much more than a hobby or occupation; it's a way of life. What gives me the motivation to derive my best creative work can be put simple: The outcome. If I create something that I do not absolutely love in the end, well, that just means I'm not done with it yet."

Justin Woomin Jeong (Steve Jobs, Abraham Lincoln)
wjeong.1@go.ccad.edu, behance.net/justwm

"Being an artist, I can express my ideas and thoughts with my own techniques and skills. I think it is amazing to see how my ideas become finalized and see outcome that I didn't expect. When I work on my design, I try to use all kinds of materials, ideas or even scenes for developing my design. As I keep putting different things together, I sometimes get inspiration from the progress."

Ashten Justus (Joseph A. Campbell)
ajustus.1@go.ccad.edu, behance.net/AJustus

"The best part about being an artist is creating things that have a purpose and make a difference. As an artist I get to make creativity a part of my everyday life, which keeps things exciting and interesting. I'm constantly learning and growing."

Alyssa Kash (John Adams, Steve Irwin, Chic Young)
kashalyssa12@gmail.com, alyssakash.com

"My favorite part of design and illustration is figuring out the aesthetic of the project. Once I figure out what I'm doing for the project. I enjoy thinking about what kind of composition, style, technique, texture, colors, and typography that I need. I have to figure out what elements best represent a company, product, label, etc."

Lindsey Kaufman (Elaine Stritch)
lindsey@heytheresquirt.com, heytheresquirt.com

"The best part about being an illustrator is seeing the positive reactions to my work; it's so delightful. I also love the camaraderie that comes with the art community. That's what I'm going to miss most about CCAD after I graduate."

Haley Kidder (Isabelle Eberhardt, Emma Goldman)
Hkidder.1@go.ccad.edu, www.HaleyKidder.com

"I am most inspired by speculative design. With this method there's a chance to communicate a what-if scenario. When given the chance to speculate we can portray a parallel world, like a novel. When we place ourselves in a story world we can better understand human relationships, society, and ourselves. This is also moment when design can convey a powerful message, critical thought, and be absurd!"

Kit Mizeres (John Zachary Young)
kitmizeresart@outlook.com, syntheticflyingmachine.com

"Metaphors have always been my main source of inspiration when illustrating. The more detail I have in an illustration, the more symbolism that lies within the often distorted and busy imagery, even if it's meant to be a personal metaphor that has sprouted from my own life associations I have experienced."

Sarah Moore (Robert Frost, Audrey Hepburn, Andy Warhol)
smoore.4@go.ccad.edu, behance.net/sarahmoore945e

"The best part about being an artist is pushing boundaries not only in my work but in other aspects of my life. My favorite thing about design and illustration is the satisfaction of creating something that others can use and enjoy."

Sunny Ngo (Philo Taylor Farnsworth)
Sunnyngo9295@gmail.com, behance.net/SunnyNgo

"I think the best part of being an artist is anything you can think of can be drawn or designed. At the same time I think it is one of the hardest parts of being an artist because sometimes you can't think or you don't know how to go about it, but if you make it through all that it feels really good to look that your end piece. "

Catherine Norwood (Queen Isabella I, Joan of Arc, Helen Keller)
cnorwood.1@go.ccad.edu, behance.net/CatherineN

"With art you have the power to express something in a more interesting way, because of this it's an incredibly powerful and beautiful tool. When we create, we're able to process the world and express our thoughts or others in a new way, and that's my favorite thing about it. Similarly, I love design and illustration because they're problem-solving tools that when used help us take these artistic expressions and ideas, and fine tune them to communicate in a way that will promote change, help others, or just make someone's day a little better."

Chris Passabet (Malcolm X)
drawn-onward@passabet.com, www.passabet.com

"The art in which you are personally invested seems to naturally be your best art. One can sense an artist's enthusiasm in a work. Chances are, if you're passionate and invested and willing to work to the limits of an idea, the final result will likely shine. This reward is my favorite thing about making art. In both illustration and design, the artist strives to amplify existing meaning through a mediation of form and content. They determine the limits of conventional communication and devise ways to speak beyond those limits."

Jonathan Pritt (Hermann Rorschach)
JPritt@jprittillustration.com, jprittillustration.com

"The fact that my name is going on my work inspires me to create the best image possible. I consider the majority of my work to be a part of me as a person, a representation in a sense, so it's of utmost importance to me to create something I'm proud to call my own."

Shane Richardson (Kellin Quinn, Erno Rubik)
srichardson.1@go.ccad.edu, behance.net/ShaneRichardson

"My favorite thing about design and illustration is actually hand lettering. Seeing as how my favorite aspect of design is typography, it makes sense because hand lettering is that awesome balance between typography and illustration. Hand lettering can really do a lot of things for a piece. Since it is literally hand done, you aren't bound to the constraints of a typeface, you can really manipulate it to whatever fits your needs which is a really nice thing to have in your skillset."

Alissa Sallah (Kazuo Umezu)
alissa@asallah.com, asallah.com

"Doing art opens up the entire world of expression and communication for me. It's something that I find liberating and exciting. The art you make is the life you live and not just the pieces you create. What's going on in the world outside of art is what inspires me the most. I always want my artwork to say something more, so my passions bleed into the content of the visual art I do. There's always something new to be seen in the world so it's great to tell people how you see it."

Alysia A. Scherger (Edgar Allan Poe)
alysia.scherger@gmail.com, behance.net/alysiascherger

"The best part about being an artist is being able to connect to someone without saying a word. It is the chance to show everyone your point of view of the world. Honestly, everyone around me inspires me to do my best work. Seeing how talented and skilled everyone else is in their own field makes me want to get better, pushing me to try harder."

Logan Schmitt (Ferdinand Von Zeppelin)
logan@loganschmitt.com, loganschmitt.com

"The best part about being an artist is being able to take a small part of your thoughts, your life, or your experiences and translate that in a unique way. My favorite thing about design and illustration is being able to communicate art in a meaningful, enlightening, and/or communicative way to benefit society and enhance our culture."

Brandon Archie Shrader (John Baird, Charles Darwin)
bshrader.1@go.ccad.edu, instagram.com/Archiier

On being an artist: "Expression, visual expression, the ability to let people see what you see gives me goosebumps. It's the base of artistry."

Cailey Tervo (Oscar Wilde)
caileytervo@gmail.com, caileytervo.com

"My favorite part of illustration is the wide diversity of styles artists can have, and the variety of applications their work can have. There is plenty of art to be inspired by, and always something new to discover. Talking with my classmates and professors, whether it is about my own illustration or theirs, is very inspiring to me. The illustration community at CCAD is positive and constructive; after a discussion with a professor I am often inspired to go back to my room and make some good work."

Shawn P. Thomas (Atilla the Hun)
STCreations@myself.com, STCreations.tumblr.com

On design: "It's a good way to cope and vent. Not just for me, but for the people who consume art for the same reasons. I can tell stories, and get inside people's heads. I can inspire and encourage, or destroy and depress. Creating entire lives and worlds. Something that myself and others can lose themselves in for a while."

Teodoro Viera (Christopher Lloyd, Freddie Mercury)
tviera.1@go.ccad.edu, behance.net/teodoroviera

"My favorite thing about design is that—obviously depending on what you work on—you can touch people's lives with it. We have a role to play in what people perceive in their environment, we're responsible for that material that surrounds them. Part of our job is to make sure that what they perceive is enjoyable, interesting, and/or meaningful."

Alicia K Weninger (Mary Shelley)
akwillustration@gmail.com, akwillustration.com

"The best part about being an artist is being able to turn your emotions and thoughts into a physical piece. My favorite thing about design and illustration is that there are so many styles and methods to achieve something, and no one has the same exact style. I'm most inspired to do my best work when there's a personal element to the work I'm doing."

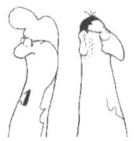

Cory Wilcox (Jim Unger)
corywilcox93@gmail.com, 3.behance.net/CoryWilcox

"My favorite thing about design and illustration is probably the whole process. I love not knowing what or how the product is going to come out, but have a sense of direction. Then finally seeing it unfold as the continuation of designing or illustrating brings the piece of art to life."

Hannah Williams (Rudyard Kipling)
hannah@hannah-m-williams.com, hannah-m-williams.com

"The best part about being an artist is that I get to make art! I love the process of working on a piece from start to finish. It's satisfying to put time and effort into making something useful and beautiful. My favorite thing about illustration and design is that they decorate our world. The books, objects, fabrics, and products we see every day are the outflow of a person's ideas and work."